S0-BMG-821

OMNIVM
LVX
CIVIVM
MDCCCLII
MDCCC
LXXVIII

Open Doorways

By the Same Author:

The Silent Explosion
Kites on a Windy Day
Summer Love and Surf
In the Twelfth Year of the War

Edited Works:

1859: Entering an Age of Crisis
Darwin
The Origin of Species
An Essay on the Principle of Population

Open Doorways

Poems by

Philip Appleman

W.W. Norton & Company, Inc.

Published simultaneously in Canada by George J. McLeod Limited, Toronto.
Printed in the United States of America.

First Edition

Grateful acknowledgment is made to the editors of the following publications, in which some of the poems in this volume first appeared. I also want to thank the National Endowment for the Arts and Indiana University for generous assistance, and my present and former students at Indiana University, Columbia University, and the State University of New York at Purchase for their friendship and inspiration, and the Grove Press for permission to use the first stanza of Andrei Voznesensky's "Taiga" (translated by Anselm Hollo) in "Poem with a First Stanza by Voznesensky." For many helpful suggestions I am indebted to Willis Barnstone, Donald Gray, Roger Mitchell, Scott Sanders, and Margie Appleman.

—P.A.

American Review: "Ten Definitions of Lifetime"
Back Door: "Afterward"
Beloit Poetry Journal: "Heart of Stone"
Chicago Tribune Sunday Magazine: "Birthday Card to My Mother," "The Girl Who Hated Threes," "Memo to the 21st Century"
College English: "Serpent," "Alive," "On the *Beagle*"
Denver Post: "Land of Cold Sun"
Harper's Magazine: "Truth," "Westhampton Cemetery"
Hawaii Review: "Scrapbook"
Indiana Writes: "Fighting the Bureaucracy"
The Literary Review: "Kicking Sea Urchins"
The Malahat Review: "For Lucia and the Black Widows of Sperlonga"
The Midwest Quarterly: "Savior"
The Nation: "Love Poem," "First Snow," "The Persistence of Memory," "Caravan"
The New England Review: "Revolution"
The New Republic: "Revision," "New Year's Resolution," "The Tennis Player Waits for What Waits for the Tennis Player"
New York Quarterly: "On a Morning Full of Sun," "Winding Down the War"
The New York Times: "Red Kite," "Waiting for the Fire"
Partisan Review: "Nobody Dies in the Spring"
Prairie Schooner: "At the End of the World"
Pulp: "Love in the Rain"
Quartet: "The Pill and the Hundred-Yard Dash"
Sewanee Review: "East Hampton: The Structure of Sound"
Southern Poetry Review: "Economics," "Central Park: The Anatomy Lesson," "Congenial Poet Desires Intense Relationship with Warm, Intelligent Poem," "Murder"
Wind: "In Two Degrees of Cold"
The Yale Review: "October Spring"

ISBN 0 393 04443 2 cloth edition
ISBN 0 393 04451 3 paper edition

1 2 3 4 5 6 7 8 9 0

for Margie: again, and always

and for my sisters:
Barbara
Ann
Sara

Contents

I *Where Light Wells Up*

Memo to the 21st Century

It was like this once: sprinklers mixed
our marigolds with someone else's phlox,
and the sidewalks under maple trees
were lacy with August shade,
and whistles called at eight and fathers walked
to work, and when they blew again,
men in tired blue shirts followed
their shadows home to grass.
That is how it was in Indiana.

Towns fingered out to country once,
where brown-eyed daisies waved a fringe on orchards
and cattle munched at clover, and
fishermen sat in rowboats and were silent,
and on gravel roads, boys and girls
stopped their cars and felt the moon and touched,
and the quiet moments ringed and focused
lakes   moon   flowers.
That is how it was
in Indiana.

But we are moving out now,
scraping the world smooth where apples blossomed,
paving it over for cars. In the spring
before the clover goes purple,
we mean to scrape the hayfield, and
next year the hickory woods:
we are pushing on, our giant diesels snarling,
and I think of you, the billions of you, wrapped
in your twenty-first century concrete,
and I want to call to you, to let you know
that if you dig down,
down past wires and pipes
and sewers and subways, you will find
a crumbly stuff called earth. Listen:
in Indiana once, things grew in it.

Nobody Dies in the Spring

Nobody dies in the spring
on the Upper West Side:
nobody dies.
On the Upper West Side
we're holding hands with strangers
on the Number 5 bus,
and we're singing the sweet
graffiti on the subway,
and kids are skipping patterns through
the bright haze of incinerators,
and beagles and poodles are making a happy
ruin of the sidewalks,
and hot-dog men are racing
their pushcarts down Riverside Drive,
and Con Ed is tearing up Broadway
from Times Square to the Bronx,
and the world is a morning miracle
of sirens and horns and jackhammers
and Baskin-Robbins' 31 kinds of litter
and sausages at Zabar's floating
overhead like blimps—oh,
it is no place for dying, not
on the Upper West Side, in springtime.

There will be a time
for the smell of burning leaves at Barnard,
for milkweed winging silky over Grant's Tomb,
for apples falling to grass in Needle Park;
but not in all this fresh new golden
smog: now there is something
breaking loose in people's chests,
something that makes butchers and bus boys
and our neighborhood narcs and muggers

go whistling in the streets—now
there is something with goat feet out there, not
waiting for the WALK light, piping
life into West End window-boxes,
pollinating weeds around
condemned residential hotels,
and prancing along at the head
of every elbowing crowd on the West Side,
singing:
Follow me—it's spring—
and nobody dies.

Land of Cold Sun

It is impossible not to be here
where light wells up from the river
to glow beneath the skin:
there is light here in the deep
center of things, in moments
of glittering truth.
But holding a moment in a pause
is stopping a river with your hands:
the slow smile
slowly fades,
the final word is spoken,
fingertips trail in the sand.
It is not enough
that the quick currents carry off pain,
that bitterness
swirls downstream;
because the sun goes cold,
because the touching is brief,
we are whispering
stop the river.

Ten Definitions of Lifetime

1

Slush, my brother said, it's
slush—the first word
I ever knew I was learning. Ankle-deep,
I shivered with cold
understanding.

2

Scout's Honor: it was another boy scout
who betrayed me—one way of finding out
what honor means.

3

At graduation, bold with endings,
I kissed her at last.
Twelve years, she said,
erasing the difference
between delay and loss.

4

When the bomb dissolved Hiroshima
every man in my company
got bombed on PX
patriotism.

5

I told the bosun:
a ship defines the ocean.
He said: horse
shit.

6

The many words for love
came easily; we would not learn the sounds
of separation.

7

In that single moment
I wanted to be immortal.
She whispered: a man who was immortal
would be as ugly
as a plastic flower.

8

All I learned in grad school
was the meaning of humility;
all I have ever forgotten
is what I learned in grad school.

9

Universe
ity: those who can, teach;
those who cannot
are the servants of teachers.

10

The poet is the unacknowledged
lexicographer of mankind.

Landing Pattern

We give them our lives
in the fog, the men with voices
out of Midwestern computers;
arms like kites, we touch
the sinister ice on the wings, our heads
always up there, forward, brains
in the cockpit, wired
to the banks of instruments, blinking
indicators, what has gone wrong
with our lives, the red lights
chattering, what is it slipping
out of our beautiful blood,
out of the ache in our marrow,
tugging us all the way home
to treetops, houses, dogs
in friendly gardens, the homely love
of grass: squeezing our eyes to feel
the solid-state components, rock
and soil, magnetic iron
moving through our veins,
mothering elements pulling
flesh to ashes:
the gentle thump,
and they've done it again, the voices
out of Midwestern
computers, brought us in
to the promises of runways,
one more perfect landing
in our beautiful blood.

Kicking Sea Urchins

All winter I read papers
on the train:
  WORLD POPULATION UP . . .
  WELFARE PROGRAM SLASHED . . .
  PRESIDENT DEFIES . . .
Consistency keeps knifing
for my heart.

In June I give up surfaces—
the sea is no mere
mirror for heaven—
black-masked, we peer through safety glass
down to the clouded past, the sun
playing ripples on our vision
of yellow rocks, spiky with black
sea urchins—deeper lie the wrecks
of old caïques, and deeper still,
the rotten ribs of Roman galleys,
fat Greek argosies,
their urns of wine crusty with
snaking shells, but resin-rich,
intact—still deeper, glowing fish
stir in the dark ooze, feeding
on blind blobs half alive,
half salt, the end and the beginning:
we grope with our antennae and nuzzle
the simple cells, mothers of
our mothers.

Pulling back to sun, we rise
again to yellow rocks, black urchins.
Careless, I jam a toe into
a fellow sea-beast: brittle spines

snap off in the toe. The pain
will pulse for days, but there will be
no festering. The spines are there
to stay.

In a cold month I fold
my *Times* with care—WATER
POLLUTION RISING IN . . . Headlines
hack at my heart, but can't
cut: I feel, inside
a glossy shoe, the secret
in my toe. Can they
suspect, these others,
respectable behind
their folded papers, that I
am full of wreckage, resined
wine, the dark of a deep
and muddy past—guess
that I have become again
one part of one percent
sea urchin?

What the U.S. Bureau of Customs Will Cry at Public Auction on June 5

The subject, sir, cannot be made poetical.
Dr. Johnson

I think that when we have got used to the steam engine, we shall not think it unpoetical.
Coventry Patmore

Poet #1:

440 Men's Wigs
2,800 Slide Rules, Two Lots
1 Steam Engine
32 Bottles Russian Champagne
500 Lbs. Oriental Hair, Assorted Lengths . . .

Poet #2:

Oriental hair?
500 pounds of it, in Customs?
Customs?—listen:
"A revolution is not a dinner party."
"Some classes triumph, others are eliminated."
"Political power grows out of the barrel of a gun."

Poet #1:

500 Lbs. Oriental Hair, Assorted Lengths
2,000 Dz. Metal Watch Bands, Four Lots
80 Lbs. Curry Powder
1 Steam Engine . . .

Poet #2:

Customs?
Just try to go home again:
you will find
little ladies in hair nets
dragging

in silver Stingrays.
Try to escape:
your passport stamped EXIT*—the belly*
refuses to go.
Try to stand still:
sand
is what water does to rock.
Try to forget:
the long siege over,
the all-clear sounding pure along the walls,
veterans jam the taverns
crying April in their beer.
Oh customs, customs, the times, the manners,
500 pounds of human hair—
supervisors, superintendents, superior officers,
stay on the job:
all the common men respect
janitor work of the intellect.

Poet #1:
Also Movie Film, Bicycles, Brassware,
Perfumes, Books, Cameras,
Religious Articles, Whiskies . . .

Poet #2:
Yes:
yes steam engines,
yes firetrucks, *yes* Stingrays, *yes*
and *yes* Hondas, paddy wagons, Greyhounds,
and *yes*
Newsweek, Harper's, Ebony, *yes,*
prosciutto, salami, braunschweiger,
Russian champagne: *yes,* it is
the crying of kids on trikes
for bales of Oriental hair,
the crying of typists with golf bags,
of welders in silver hats—it is

the customs, the summing-up, the crying
of lots, across
chasms of inventories, range
upon range of rusting
steam engines;
it is how we buy and sell,
barter our needs,
arrange our Order,
Control:
the way we live our lives, love
our loves in the lots of lives about us,
the loves, the lives, the loves,
that happy crying.

On the *Beagle*

There are men who hold the world
in their fingertips and
are part of what they hold.

The *Beagle* set sail
to easy summer—five years on sea
and land the watchful man
from Cambridge put
his fingers on a universe
of cuttlefish, sea-slugs, condors,
the ancient monsters' bones,
megatherium, mastodon: all
fixed forever in immutable forms, creatures
of a benign
Intelligence.
It was written.

And yet . . .

The young man put his fingers on
the pulse of rivers, coral reefs,
pampas and mountains,
the flotsam of earthquakes—and
on futures of learning, from
pigeons' plumage, the beaks of finches, bones
of rabbits and ducks—decades
of learning,
dissecting ten thousand
barnacles—pondering:
"If
we choose to let
conjecture run wild, then animals—
our fellow brethren in pain,
disease, death, suffering, and famine—
they may partake from our origin

in one common ancestor:
we may be all
netted together."

The *Beagle* labored on: in the winter
of Cape Horn,
twenty-three days of beating
against the icy bluster
came to broken boats
and spoiled collections.
The good ship rode to shelter—
and there on a rocky point
of Tierra del Fuego, naked
in snow, a mother
suckled her child
("whilst the sleet fell and thawed
on her naked bosom, and on the skin
of her naked baby")—there, in a little band,
stood
"man in his primitive wildness,"
ringed by the dark beech forest:
"As they threw their arms wildly
around their heads,
their long hair streaming,
they seemed the troubled spirits
of another world."
There
in the Bay of Good Success,
Charles Darwin, on the foredeck of the *Beagle*,
our future in his freezing fingertips,
stared into the faces
of our past.

October Spring

When crisp catalpa leaves
come tumbling down the frosty morning air
like tarpaulins for tulips,
it's spring again in little college towns,
October snipping at our brave beginnings,
the new year pruned away to nine lean months
of three-day weeks and fifty-
minute hours. This new year lights
no dogwood, no magnolia to find us
limping through our shrunken moments or
calling courage from our stubborn past,
the long pilgrimage of algae,
sponges, reptiles, flowers,
men. No robins linger
in the haze of this late spring
to whistle, in our fifty-minute hours,
the miracles to come: birds
of brighter plumage, richer songs,
flowers in subtler shades, men and women
walking together in peace.
But the big catalpa leaves
float crippled down the slanting sun,
brown nourishment to our long
hope, and we are clinging to
our thinning years because brown leaves
are clumsy promises: because it's
spring again.

The Pill and the Hundred-Yard Dash

The feel of it, deep:
hairy half-humans hurtling through trees,
Cro-Magnon tracking antelope,
galloping bandits in badlands—

sprint
the dig and pull
and heart
striding out, crying
blood to a million
years, lungs
howling the race, the race,
the furious driving thighs,
blind and sweet and
f l o a t
on the easy coming strides and
sprint
and the heart, the lungs, the
thighs, the throb in the tips of toes,
hot spray in the muscles
and
there, *there,*
the tug at the chest,
grateful pull of the lungs,
heart,
thighs relaxed
and

this:

that afterward
there is nothing—
only the mute
majesty
of the thing
itself.

Bicentennial: The Course of Empire

Looking westward: and there,
brimming over with sunrise,
the towers and magic casements
of Jersey, then
the continent itself—happy valleys,
two cars in every garage, hog
butcher to the world, pioneers,
o pioneers. That first step
beyond the Hudson stamped out
the stone age, brought empire
to the grasslands: squint,
and you can see from here
farmers on their tractors
breaking up the territories, sea
to shining sea—look again: in the Napa Valley
barefoot peasants are stomping
tubs of grapes, tribute to the emperor
standing here looking westward where
Kawasaki's roaring the Machine Age
in again by the back door, and just beyond,
small brown women are hustling
tires for Yellow Cabs, and farther on,
Greeks with torsos like marble
are casting bronze ballots for the Articles
of Confederation,
and Frenchmen are dreaming up statues
of *liberté*, and
somewhere in Spain,
caravels set sail to the unknown waters.
Empire is a curling vision: look
again, you will see
the back of your own head, looking west,
and seeing, o pioneer,
the back of your own head
looking west.

Fighting the Bureaucracy

Have we tacked and beaten everywhere now,
run before the wind on friendly swells,
waded ashore on unknown reefs
bearing greetings, messages,
the voices of our people—only
to be fogged in here at last,
waiting?
Beyond this mush of cloud
it all goes on, the secret talks,
negotiations, flash bulbs
in the corridors; the enemy
touches official forms
with fingertips; we watch him
turn to sip coffee,
glance at the clock.
Waiting, waiting, we shuffle our feet,
jingle coins in pockets,
finger the buttons on coats—
and remember a silvery wake in the sea,
a golden doubloon of sun, dolphins
racing the foam through warm green light,
galleons standing to lee.
The long line inches forward:
fog goes sifting away like night,
and we sing at the bow of our dreams.

New Year's Resolution

Well, I did it again, bringing in
that infant Purity across the land,
welcoming Innocence with gin
in New York, waiting up
to help Chicago,
Denver, L.A., Fairbanks, Hon-
olulu—and now
the high school bands are alienating Dallas,
and girls in gold and tangerine
have lost all touch with Pasadena,
and young men with muscles and missing teeth
are dreaming of personal fouls,
and it's all beginning again, just like
those other Januaries in
instant replay.

But I've had enough
of turning to look back, the old
post-morteming of defeat:
people I loved but didn't touch,
friends I haven't seen for years,
strangers who smiled but didn't speak—failures,
failures. No,
I refuse to leave it at that, because
somewhere, off camera,
January is coming like Venus
up from the murk of December, re-
virginized, as innocent
of loss as any dawn. Resolved: this year
I'm going to break my losing streak,
I'm going to stay alert, reach out,
speak when not spoken to,
read the minds of people in the streets.
I'm going to practice every day,
stay in training, and be moderate
in all things.
All things but love.

"Your Papers, Please"

It always took me by surprise,
that abrupt request, blunt
as a fist: Paul Henreid, say, on a perilous
mission for the Resistance, or Charles Boyer,
off to some splendid sabotage
for Freedom—then
suddenly the flashlight, the bullying badges, and
"Vos papiers, s'il vous plaît"—and damn
if they didn't have them, every time,
passport-size, official—faked,
of course, but irresistibly
official, all
prim in their stamps
and numbers.
Nobody over here had numbers then,
or papers: astonishing, that notion
that you always carried around with you
your Identity.
Well,
the War changed all that. (*You* know
which war, the one where Henreid
and Boyer led us to victory, their papers
and numbers intact as armor.)
"Private Doe, 15345219, reporting, sir"—
you got used to it then, your number,
like learning your own name, your face in the mirror;
and never in your sprawling life would you ever
forget it—it was
your number.
Later we learned, They
had our numbers, too—the old
Social Security digits showing up
unexpectedly, like relatives on holidays

(Private Citizen Doe, 309-20-4763, reporting, sir)
—not just on the job,
but at school, on tax forms,
licenses, passports
(U.S. Citizen Doe, F1008541, reporting, sir)
—and somehow, before we knew it,
the numbers were there in the swivel chairs,
barking out orders, and
all of *us* had sort of
dwindled. Oh, we're still
around, of course, but only in practice,
not in principle: our muffled names, our shadowy
faces in mirrors have no such
authenticity
as our Blue Cross Benefit Code, 5T7W8,
or our First National Account, 22 0433 2
or even our area code, 812
or our zip code, 47401, reporting,
sir, reporting, sir.
Still, we hug
the memory of other
identities, a land where there are no papers,
where faces move through the streets
unnumbered, where we can sing
the chaotic music of catbirds,
walk the meandering streams, drift
in cumulus, shifting
from camels to weasels to whales, drink
from unmetered springs,
and taste the unweighed apples, the price-
less pears.

Seeing into Bedrooms

The naked eye sees only
naked flesh, lovers in their ageless
poses, the awkward elegance
of thigh on thigh: the eye
is not enough.

A 7-by-30 Tecnar
zooms to the bedside—bellies touching
call the night to witness: this
is more than a simple act, more than just
the pleasure of skin—but
something somehow foggy,
blurred.
The 8-by-40 Leitz
makes matters clearer: beads of sweat
glisten on rosy breasts—but
this thing in the glasses is no
brief seesaw of passion, these lips
on their warm adventures
to the secret places of love;
there is in it all, behind it, some
sense of loss in the act of winning,
fog in the back of the eyes.
The 10-by-50 Zeiss
trembles in the hand, the field of vision
dwindles to details of movement:
mouth on mouth, pink nipples trembling, the slow
slide of muscle and blood—pieces
of a puzzle as big as sight, still
blurred.

The last attempt: eyes
shut tight, it all comes in-
to focus—slithering shapes
of jealousy, loss, chances missed,

old loves undead—consumed
in the rhythm of hips,
spasms in thighs driving
gray chimeras out
of bedrooms, leaving the tight
mystery of love made visible
in the glaring dark
under the eyelids.

Handwriting on a Wall

1

Graffito:
"And God said . . ."
The trouble began with that.

2

Lovers:
every moment is a sharp edge,
beginning
and ending.

3

Egotists:
from the fortieth floor
there are no giants on earth.

4

Moralists:
there are always
more bathers on sand
than in water.

5

Poets:
diesels make songs
in their own dark
language.

6

Critics:
no snake has ever
successfully
swallowed its own tail.

7

Extremists:
for every Scylla
there's a Charybdis.

8

Capitalists:
pigeons own everything.

9

Revolutionaries:
the stormiest beach
cleans its own face like a cat.

10

Intellectuals:
at the death of cities
the roofs go first.

11

Pessimists:
dying farmers leave behind
plowshares and
the earth.

12

Optimists:
the good Lord planned it this way:
corpses face down in the mud.

13

Graffito:
"The God you worship
is the god you deserve."

East Hampton: The Structure of Sound

Bedrooms ease their shingles
into the yawning gardens:
the silence sucks at my eardrums
and my skull flowers open like popcorn.
Perpetual Sunday morning:
the quiet spreads out like a meadow.
I loaf and invite my soul,
and it sprawls in the shade like a toadstool.

Mondays, Manhattan is shapely
in the perfect circles of sirens,
the shrill music of taxis
making symmetries, patterns, and bounds:
jackhammers chisel my brain
to correct community standards
as the dawn comes up like thunder
out of Brooklyn, the shaper of sunrise.

II *Backs to the Wall*

Truth

We shall die alone.
Pascal

An army of moments:
jade against the skin
heavenly Aïda
a view of Toledo
belly and thighs—
it is always
war to the last man,
every man
is the last man,
you
are the last man
remembering
heat and pressure
mass and energy
wave length and frequency
beauty and truth—
none of your captains
will remember,
non of your non-coms
will follow you there,
only the big-eyed recruits:
sunrise in April
purple clowns Beaujolais
duckling in peaches
rose leaves and rain—
at the final moment
they
will be with you, blindfolded
with you, standing there with
you, backs to the wall.

Westhampton Cemetery

founded 1795

for Jim and Tanya

No place for elegies, in these stern
stones, bleached
by the misty light that haloes gulls
and weathers the gray shingles
of the Hamptons—no elegies, but grace:
Blessed are the dead
which die in the Lord: my flesh
will rest in hope.
No place for elegies in this austere
devotion to joy, the faith
of the departed:
They do not die nor lose
their mortal sympathy,
nor change to us, although
they change.
No elegies for Mehitable, wife
of Enoch Jagger, died
1799 in the twenty-fifth
year of her age;
for Warren Goodall, drowned at Fire Island,
1832;
for Jennie McCue, died 1871,
aged three years, nine days—no
elegies, but grace:
Precious in the sight of the Lord
is the death of His Saints: we sorrow not
as those which have no hope.

But for the backs that wearied out
these scars in the pale earth,
and for sailors at the aching capstans,
for fishermen scanning
the ashy sky—elegies,

yes, for all
of these—for bonneted girls
stooping till sundown in the itch
of potato fields, new widows walking their roofs
for the overdue whalers,
maids in the faded Hamptons
staring at hope chests—elegies,
chiseled in mossy stone:
From sorrow, toil and pain
and sin we shall be free.
This misty light is an elegy
for the living:
bleaching our blood to water,
scaling our bone to chalk,
fading every morning song
to the minor of farewell.

Serpent

The delicate backbone smashed,
it lived till sundown; then
its mate came for revenge.
The long muscle
glistened:
"Your eyes shall be opened,
you shall be
as gods, knowing good
and evil."

"You are no snake,"
she told him. "You
are pure superstition—go
hypnotize a bird
or suck the milk from goats. Go,
or I'll give *you* a backache, too."

He slithered off, limp as liver,
swearing to find some weaker time
out there in the orchard,
and the storms he would conjure then
would wreck that greenery
and stand a guard there, blazing,
with a sword.

Revision

Why do I always see
the death in things?
Squinting in the sun, I notice
beach umbrellas sliding off,
one by one, to wet sand, waves
chopping up, full of purple tentacles,
December storms;
my cloudy look turns budding leaves to mulch,
breaks up moaning lovers,
peels the ruddy paint
from Indiana barns.

Prudence is a killing frost;
Providence poisons the soil;
Wisdom, always moving on, leaves
a brown track in the grass.

I will close my eyes and hope for
some lucky drift of jasmine,
low voices, and a dumb
trembling in the groin.

The Tennis Player Waits for What Waits for the Tennis Player

In the slippery swelter of asphalt,
in a blistering backhand return,
you wait every June, every August
for that stabbing of fate in the elbow,
that first sharp knifing of fact;
and because it comes with a certain
smug angle of the sun,
and because it comes with a bird
turning transparent as truth,
and because it comes with a cry
like preaching in the wind—
you know you are becoming
one of the pure, pale
Others; and you call back
all the grubby friends
of childhood, and command them
to surround your skin with singing.

Red Kite

Onto that long snowing of sand
the sea had nudged another derelict,
red as the rising sun in smog, and sheer
as butterflies, kite string and all,
ready to fly.
And it would have been a perfect
gift from the green tide, if
I hadn't, that day, in the idle-
ness of beaches, chucked
a stone at a silver
foraging fish—
and hit him, dead
center.
He leaped,
in a twisting flash of belly-white
so much like human pain I caught my breath
an ugly moment—then
the fish swam on, as graceful as before.
It was only that one
numbing
moment,
the terrible lifetime wait
as the fishflash in the air
meant quick or dead—how can I put it—
annihilation
hung there in the wind,
and a kite from the sea bled
red pain across the sky.

Central Park: The Anatomy Lesson

The bones of the skeleton move
like levers;
muscles attach to the bones
by means of tendons, and contract
to clench fists, or deliver
a blow to the face.
When two muscles act in concert,
like the flexors and extensors of the leg
sending a knee to the groin
it is called synergism.
The metacarpal bones of the hand
form a united mass with the bones of the wrist
and are suitable for quick
chops to the neck or kidneys.
The calcaneum, or heel bone, is the largest
bone of the tarsus; it
can in most cases crush
the thoracic cage
(notably the false or floating ribs)
in a single stomp.
Of the various bones of the skull,
the occipital, with its egg-shell contour,
is the most vulnerable
to blunt objects like the tire wrench
or jack handle.

That's all for now. Repeat this lesson
till you have it
by heart.
Tomorrow night we shall consider
the circulatory system: the jugular
and other veins.

Caravan

It is a hazy dream, this town,
the white walls, the minarets,
the twisting cobblestone alleys:
you see yourself in the small bazaars,
haggling with wrinkled men for silk and silver,
sipping glasses of hot mint tea
in the perfume of kif and saffron.
The amazing thing is, it is true:
once upon a time you are here
among faceless women in kaftans,
old men dry as sand,
boys with the fingers of forty thieves.
But the thing you did not expect
is the eyes; these eyes were not in the dream.
They peer at you over veils
and out of the gloom of the souq:
windows of the soul, they tell you
lust, envy, gluttony, greed,
and all the homely virtues;
and the eyes you will never forget
are the milky blind eyes of children,
the charcoal rage of the woman
who hates you because you were born,
and the brown pity of that one man
who helps you when you call out.
There is no magic carpet to take you
where these eyes no longer exist;
for a thousand and one black nights
you will wake to that staggering dream.

Revolution

When she came on, straight,
skin silky
black, her eyes a black
bonfire, I felt
my eyes go paler: ice-
blue,
Arctic gray—felt
my hair turn silver, skin
cellophane—
felt flesh and bone
eddying in x-rays, the air
opening up to swallow—and
I grabbed for things, the brown
table, black chairs, ebony
piano—but too
late, I had already faded into
the white shine
of the walls.

Message

Paris: there are pigeons,
dark alleys, pale skin.
Camus

On the windows, the windows,
this strange yellow rain,
and the soggy clock ticking: we
have defined ourselves candlesticks,
jiggers of gin
and photos and bookends and
beakers of bourbon:
the telephone
never rings.

In this yellow rain, miles
are consistently one-point-six-oh-nine
kilometers long and the temperature
varies from thirty-three F
to one degree C
at twenty-nine inches of mercury falling,
and the dripping calendar
flips its pages, and yellow rain
washes away another month
and the telephone
never rings.

Pigeons in dark alleys
wait for sun: we rub ourselves skin-deep
with tanning lotion and wait;
you are five-feet-five, a stately
queen of gin and I
am one-point-seven-eight meters tall
in my pale bare feet, one of the bourbon
kings, and we wait
for sun in the yellow rain
while the telephone
goes on never
ringing.

Poem with a First Stanza by Voznesensky

Your teeth are brave,
they smile like a knife,
your golden eyes
buzz like bees

and your thighs are sincere,
they twine like curses,
your elegant arms
clamp me in fear

and your milky-blue breasts
are souring my juices,
your hungry crevices
gorging like quicksand.

As your golden eyes
sting me with honey,
your brave smile gouges
sweet holes in my heart.

Afterward

In the morning it was no better:
the chrysanthemums had frosted gray
and snow was beating the robin's nest
to splinters, in the memory
of screams.

Think
of a slash of light in lace curtains,
a solitary gnat delirious, spinning
in sun his small ecstasy—think
of the names of girls, gentle
as the melody of fountains—think
of children rubbing sleepy
eyes and stretching—think
of the flash of sea birds,
milkweed flying,
picnic tables in the shifting shade.

November wind is hissing in
apple trees run wild;
in the ruined stones of cities, boys
are boarding buses in uniform,
mothers standing
stiff in their black coats
moaning
the pain of staying alive.

Because
we never love enough,
cannot say we do,
counting the slow ticks to five o'clock, the gin
screaming like wind
in the broken flowers.

For Lucia and the Black Widows of Sperlonga

I

They drift in whitewashed doorways, dark
shadows, tending it all: no sparrow
falls but they observe, and tally.
The village stirs under their solemn gaze:
squid and shrimp bring
flies to market, espresso
steams beneath the lone
tree
in the toy piazza,
figs and olives swell in deep July
on the slope to the shore
where men are mending nets, their big toes poking.

July is kodachrome Sperlonga: aliens
sweep across the piazza like
surf—Germans with blue-
eyed kids, Parisian mannequins squinting in blue
sunglasses, Americans in blue
jeans. They buy day-old
Le Mondes and *Herald Tribunes* and
pose in blue
bikinis on the sand, a fairy tale
of beach umbrellas.
July Sperlonga is the sweet
life that alien, Tiberius,
came for: sun, exotic fish
and flesh, orgies of blue.

September: the XXth century
retreats to Rome. Fishnet
curtains ripple in the autumn doorways,
black women on whitewash
tighten the wrinkles of their eyes

and rule again, in whispers.
The warm September Sunday Lucia walked
with Tonio to the hills and pagan grotto, dark
whispers passed along the stairstep streets,
the ashes of ancient eyes
flickered: *fallen, fallen.*

Shy creature mocked by whistles at the cafe,
by catcalls in the streets, Lucia
found no friend no priest no parent
strong as the dark old women and the whispers.
She held alone
her blackness.
In bright October sun
they found her where her farmer father kept
the poisons, her slender light
extinguished: Doctor Rinaldi
pronounced her
Pure.

As pure as Italian melodrama:
life follows art.

Dark women of villages:
in the unswept corners of the soul
are furry spiders.

II

Forty hazy winters married:
holding out again till morning chugs
with fishing boats, twinkling back
to dawn and shore and scampi-scented bed,
then setting out to mist and spray,
slapping sheets on stone at shoreside,
forty winters down and up

two hundred rocky stairsteps
jiggling tubs of sheets
on knotted hair, home to pasta brewed
in witches' kettles, floury wheels
of black bread, olive oil, the feel
of clumsy bellies,
forty winters of *ragazzi* kicking
soccer in the winding streets, of nursing
life in a treeless town to window pots,
forty winters married.

(In summer, always the aliens—
blondes in naked blue bikinis
slithering sleek bronze hips,
scorching the lounging fishermen
with heat not of Sperlonga they
brought with them to bed like panting goats
on August afternoons.)

Forty winters: parents, children dead,
shutting off the light for one full year,
patches of black across the past—
until that moonless night of logic
(what will be, will be)
when high winds tease a little boat
like kittens swatting butterflies
and *basta:*
one more widow in Sperlonga, taking
black as permanent
as brides of Jesus.

Dark women: in the tight web of Sperlonga
can anyone spin thoughts
that are not spiders?

III

Tiberius lingers in
his marble grotto, but
there are no shadows of the modern Caesar
who lost all battles, and the war.
Nazis didn't trust him to defend
even Sperlonga on its little perch
above the sea: gave the villagers one hour
to leave their whitewashed homes. They
froze for nine months
in the hills, praying *alla Vergine*
and dying *à la* Darwin, weakest first—the meek
inherit nothing from mother
nature.

A ruined bunker
three feet thick with concrete:
"7–26–44" someone has scrawled in red.
Victories came hard in these hills, every hump
took pounds of flesh—mountains, mud,
the thump of 88's,
red oozings in the rain—
but on 7–26–44
the bunker splintered at the touch
of red-eyed men.
The assault force was motley:
Americans, Brazilians, French, Moroccans
famous for two things: savagery
and rape.
When they found the Sperlonghesi in the hills,
no one escaped, the women (even
old women in black) too few—
Sperlonga is small, an army large—
the assault was universal, classic:

children, old men, everyone—the victors
violated, ravished, defiled, possessed
the villagers.
No one in these white streets
has breathed it aloud
since 7–26–44—but
before Lucia was born in Sperlonga,
there was an orgy in these hills
Tiberius would have wondered at.

And now to see a boy and girl
go hand in hand in the pagan, fruitless hills—
well,
it is no simple idyll in
the twisting stairway streets,
in the secret memories of
old women in black.

IV

It is a fairy-tale village,
fit for bedtime stories: there is
a Good Lorenzo here, and a Bad Lorenzo,
a Good Milk-Lady and a Bad Milk-Lady,
a Good Beach and a Bad Beach,
and so on. The people are
charming on Sundays,
all smiles and *buon giorno*'s, they walk
the extra mile with weary strangers.

"Mondays," a friend
murmurs to me in the Good Cafe in the Good Piazza
under the stare of dark women
in doorways behind fishnet screens
on balconies in windows:

"Mondays the place
is a nest of spiders. Lucia,
you know, was beaten by her father
when the whispers came, faded in her mother's
bitterness. But after the suicide
and the doctor's fact to prop their little faith,
the parents breathed indignant righteousness
and sued the woman who first
said *fallen*—just to make a fast
lira from Lucia's lonely virtue. Only
in villages," he says,
"do you find the real, the true
depravities."

"Is it fair?" I ask him. "What about
the Good Milk-Lady, the Good Lorenzo . . ."
Eyes half closed, he mutters,
"Yes. And there is a Good Church here
and a Bad Church, yes—but listen: old women kneel
by dozens in the Bad Church,
nodding while the black priests chant.
The Good Church is boarded up: that
is your fairy-tale Sperlonga.
Ciao."

He left, in a sunny evening shower
as a rainbow wrapped the village,
one end in a tomato patch,
the other in the blue shallows.
The pot of gold in tomatoes was
already known, and mortgaged; and before
the kids got down to the beach,
a sleek yacht skimmed in from nowhere good
and anchored right into the treasure.
That, my hard-nosed friend would say,
is what happens to fairy tales.

Alive

Uncle Jimmie had a hunch that cancer,
the rat that gnawed away behind his ears,
was part of the warm earth and silver woods
and snowy meadows in the mountains. Surgeons
stabbed at the rat: scalpels sliced away
the ears one April dawn, as catbirds,
perched in the morning treetops, mocked the calling
of cardinals. Stabbed and missed—the rat survived.
The day they clipped out Uncle Jimmie's cheeks
and upper lip, he pondered artichokes,
truffles, and a certain Tuscan wine.
And when they snipped his nose, he wept for roses
and the fresh sea breeze—and thought a while, and played
his hunch: *Stop cutting,* Jimmie told them, *let*
me go to earth and snow and silver trees.

But the rat kept gnawing, and Auntie Flo went on
reading St. Paul (*The works of the flesh are uncleanness*),
and praying, and paying the bills—and the surgeons huddled,
frowning at Jimmie's want of reverence
for faith and modern medicine. With skillful
suturing, they lifted out his tongue
and dropped the wagging muscle in a pail,
and Uncle Jim, who used to murmur quatrains
out of Omar, kept his peace. Still, his eyes
kept pleading: *Stop the cutting, let me go*
to earth and silver trees! But Jimmie knew
the rat would work in just behind his eyes,
and Auntie Flo would go on reading Paul
(*They that are Christ's have crucified the flesh*)
and praying, and paying the bills—and the pale blue eyes
would have to go: one Sunday after Angelus, Jim began
his dark forgetting of the green
wheat fields, red hills in the sun,

and how the clouds drive storms across the sea.
Some Monday following, a specialist
trimmed away one-quarter of his brain
and left no last gray memory of Omar
or snowy fields   or earth   or silver trees.

But Uncle Jimmie lives: the rat lies quiet now,
and tubes lead in and out of Jimmie's veins
and vents. Auntie Flo comes every day
to read to bandages the Word Made Flesh,
and pray, and pay the bills, and watch with Jimmie,
whittled down like a dry stick, but living:
the heart, in its maze of tubes, pumps on,
while catbirds mock the calling of cardinals,
artichokes grow dusty green in sunshine,
butterflies dally with the roses,
and Uncle Jimmie is no part of these.

Train Whistles

They'd howl us out of childhood dreams
like old dogs mad at the moon,
and I'd lie awake in the summer dark,
thinking *the sounds of night*
are messages of death,
and feeling the rails that split the state,
projecting visions of New York,
Chicago, necessary evils
for the ends of Indiana roads;
in midnight eyelids I could see
the twinkling cars, portable
fairylands, with names
like Golden West and Silver City,
rattling through the corn fields, past
our shadowy elms and lacy
spindled porches, carrying
tired men home to lonely women
in Fort Wayne, South Bend,
Kendallville.

Out there in the dark Midwest
they're whistling coal and cattle now,
not salesmen in the smoky club cars,
young men off to battle
with the cities.
Are the somber voices of our past
calling now to someone else's future—
a generation on,
will aging children hear again
that long moaning in the dark,
remembering
the messages of night?

Murder

Who was it standing there
while you slept? There's
a taste on the tip of the tongue
like bitter almonds, and off
in the corner of the eye
someone is slipping into dusk
at the edge of the room, and something
without a face
is chasing you through the woods, your legs
rooted like stumps,
your screaming strangled to whimpers, and
you know in the lump of your heart
that the faceless thing
is yourself, it is
man and wife slamming doors,
in the dregs of every cup
a trace of arsenic—it is rage
at the boss, feeling
in the palm of the hand
the thump of lead pipe—it is
the fury of neighbors, the tang
of gunpowder, smell
of quicklime eating flesh; you
breathe it in with the morning
coffee, the pleasant drone
of mowing lawns,
in every blade of grass
the open razor.

You wrench yourself out of nightmare
and open your eyes
in time to see the bludgeon crashing down
and the face above it, roaring
with your laughter.

At the End of the World

Remember the quiet time
an hour before the sun, the sea
lapping silent beaches:
think of men in deerskins chipping
mussels from the yellow rocks;
think of red men camping where
rivers ran pure through pines
to the flickering sea.

Spin the globe, it's all
L.A.: freeways racing
down to Rio,
smog along the Congo, neon
screaming in Mongolia, and
Fords, eight abreast, crashing
through the Taj.

Still they are prophesying not
a quick apocalypse, only
more of the same:
Behold how the wicked flourish,
they are chanting in Nineveh,
Woe, woe to our cities
staggers the streets of Babylon.

Bittersweet lasts out the winter,
clocks tick on like gods,
a kiss is still warm on my neck,
and in a glory of guilty
joy, I hear
my own voice
singing, singing.

III *Something Is Gone*

On a Morning Full of Sun

One of our gulls
is keening in the flat
blue light: *something*
is gone, is gone, is gone—a hundred
teen-age boys picked out
of mud, zipped into
plastic bags, and air-mailed
home to Mom.

White wings sweep over our beach
in formation: straw huts leap
into flame—*something*
is gone, is gone—
I stagger up the sand,
press my M-16
to the skull of a peasant girl,
and watch the bone
go chipping off and dancing
through the flat blue keening
air.

The Persistence of Memory

We have been through them now, the silver
anniversaries: VE-Day,
the Bomb, the wreck
of Japan, all
misted in quaintness—and still
they keep coming,
brown women swirling past,
the armies somewhere behind them, burning
the villages: always the same,
the same weary women each year,
muddy skeletons lugging
the brass pots, tugging the delicate children,
camping in culverts, eating grass—
and the rich bombers run
on their shabby targets; kids
in helmets inch
through torn jungles; somewhere at sea,
ships lob shells
at the horizon—it is all a memory
of old men:
the brave planes limping home,
balding heroes sending
their sons to glory, the bleeding
always the same, like father
like son, breastplate
and buckler rusting
in a dream of blood we
move through, open-eyed,
sons of our dreaming fathers,
waiting for all the memories
to fade.

Winding Down the War

and this is it: the pause,
right hand to the sun,
the glare of crazed mirrors
in the sea, hopelessly
beautiful;

this is the end of it:
a long gray glare on stumps
moldy yet from some
old, inadequate flood;
G.I.'s slicing the ears
off muddy corpses;
upstream, a thousand
hulls in mothballs, waiting
the howl, the call again
to fear on the glittering water;
the flicker of orange flames
on Main Street;
sad-mouthed harlequins
manning the pumps and hoses; and

this is it: the pause,
hand over eyes, the glare,
the desert sea

Peace with Honor

Solitudinem faciunt,
pacem appellant.

I

The outer provinces are never secure:
our Legions hold the camps, their orders
do not embrace the minds
and hearts of barbarians. So, when the late-
late news reported the outlandish
screams in that distant temple,
the great bronze Victory toppled,
red stains in the sea, corpses
stranded by the ebb tide—all of that,
and only four hundred
armed men at the garrison—why,
of course it had to come, the massacre,
the plundering.

II

It was the decade's scandal at home,
the humiliation, the Eagles gone.
Senators put on grim faces
and gossiped over Bloody
Marys—what laureled head would roll for this?
Reports from the field
were cabled not to the Emperor but
to the Joint Chiefs, to filter
through at last, edited
and heavy with conclusions: the traitor,
they revealed, was not in uniform,
the treason was our own permissiveness;
in sterner times our Fathers would not
have suffered such dishonor.
We nodded: yes, they knew,

the Chiefs, what ancient virtue was.
The twilight shudders of matrons
seasoned our resolution. Somber, we took
a fourth martini, wandered to the couches,
the tables rich with peacocks' tongues,
and nodded,
nodded, waiting.

III

They sent our toughest
veterans, the Ninth Legion, the Fourteenth,
the Hundred-and-First, their orders un-
ambiguous: teach the barbarians respect.
Our marshals chose the spot: a steep defile
covering the rear, our regular troops drawn close,
light-armed auxiliaries at their flanks,
cavalry massed on the wings.
The enemy seethed everywhere, like a field
of wind-blown grasses.
There were the usual
harangues, the native leaders boasting
their vast numbers, screaming
freedom or death;
our generals, with that subtle sneer
they learn at the Academy,
pointing only to the Eagles on their tall shafts—
and every man remembered
the shame of Eagles fallen, comrades' bones
unburied: there was that curious thing,
men in bronze and steel, weeping.
And then the charge, the clash of arms,
cavalry with lances fixed, the glorious
victory: a hundred thousand tons of TNT
vaporized their villages, their forests were
defoliated, farmland poisoned forever,
the ditches full of screaming children,
target-practice for our infantry.
The land, once green and graceful,

running with pleasant streams in the rich brown earth,
was charred and gutted—not even a bird
would sing there again.

IV

A glorious victory, of course,
but in a larger sense, a mandatory act
of justice: the general peace
was kept, the larger order held; peasants
for a thousand leagues around
are working their mules again.
Our prisoners and Eagles all returned,
we dine at the rich tables,
thinking of the Sunday games,
thinking of anything but rebellion—thinking
the honor of Empire
is saved.

Waiting for the Fire

Not just the temples, lifting
lotuses out of the tangled trees,
not the moon on cool canals,
the profound smell of the paddies,
evening fires in open doorways,
fish and rice the perfect end of wisdom;
but the small bones, the grace, the voices like
clay bells in the wind, all wasted.
If we ever thought of the wreckage
of our unnatural acts,
we would never sleep again
without dreaming a rain of fire:
somewhere God is bargaining for Sodom,
a few good men could save the city; but
in that dirty corner of the mind
we call the soul
the only wash that purifies is tears,
and after all our body counts,
our rape, our mutilations,
nobody here is crying; people who would weep
at the death of a dog
stroll these unburned streets dry-eyed.
But forgetfulness will never walk
with innocence; we save our faces
at the risk of our lives, needing
the wisdom of losses, the gift of despair,
or we could kill again.
Somewhere God is haggling over Sodom:
for the sake of ten good people
I will spare the land.
Where are those volunteers
to hold back the fire? Look:
when the moon rises over the sea,
no matter where you stand
the path of the light comes to you.

IV *The Telling of the Heart*

Love Poem

The lonely pull of blood
at midnight: capillaries
seeping slow in firm
flesh—a closed system.

Touching: the thrill of cool
skin, sing-song of
her breath, the gurgle
of many yards of tubing
somewhere deep, and
always the thump, thump
of her tough heart.

Ars Poetica

Think of it, nine thousand
breakfasts together, and now
coffee again for the first time: what
a virginal movement it is, this
silvering together, every day
the very first day, every night
the first night, not a film replayed, more
like pages in a long book, strata
in these limestone hills we live in,
two billion years old.
We're not yet as old as the limestone,
but we're catching up—or rather,
reducing the proportion, like a kid brother
gaining on his elders; we're gaining
on the limestone and
beginning to see
it's an art, like Cellini's, this
silvering—like poetry, reminding us
in its earnest, nagging way,
that every new minute we risk
immortality, surviving
for nine thousand days by luck or cunning;
but at the end we're sent to press
with all our typos intact, fossils, captive
in the ancient rock. Meanwhile,
we're all such fumblers, gauche,
all thumbs: maybe
poems and marriages deal
mostly in failures—on the way to shape,
nine thousand blemishes hitching a ride. Maybe
only a poem or a silver bowl
will tell us as well as love: that
these are the only raw
materials we have—the painful

moments of wonder,
the small, well-meant betrayals, rain
in the limestone hills.
Well, we're not finished yet;
the revisions are still in process, a line here,
a day there, the whole thing
taking on a kind of polished
mutilation, a scarred silver florin,
a weathered hill,
an epic fragment.
There's time yet to get it—not right,
of course, but anyway revised,
emended, more mature
in its lumpy way. Think of it,
two billion years of shaping:
it's a beginning.

The Girl Who Hated Threes

At the beach
she always took my hand
as though we were sophomores again,
or as though a wave might race in like
some wild Greek myth
and sweep her out to sea—
but of course it wasn't that;
she took my hand
to pair the two of us off
against the world. She hated threes,
didn't believe in the Trinity,
wouldn't read trilogies or listen to trios
or type in triplicate.

But all that came to me late,
late one winey evening,
with a Burgundy sun going down
and a Rhinish full moon rising,
came to me in that swimming twilight, as
she took my hand again:
that the rhythm of love is always
a pulsing of two's—and in
the dawn of that twilight vision,
the reeling gulls paired off, crabs
staggered the sand all twinned,
and a brace of boozy bluefish
leaped and carried on
as her stubborn grip held
wax and wane,
ebb and flood—and all the beautiful
barbarians drifting on that twilight beach
paired off in a tug
of give and take,
lose and hold—
and the summer tides went on in the image of love:
in and out,
in and out.

Savior

It is a troll's morning with bells,
chimes of Black Mass under my eyelids,
every morning my body found
floating in formaldehyde, bearing
bruises that don't show,
the trolls clubbing me all night,
smashing nerves;
a shadow of myself comes
at me, whiskered, eyes
pickled in brine, mouth a swamp
of last night's beer, the sun
stuck somewhere in clouds, everything
outside gray, the grass dead as a mummy—
even the ground is dirty,
dusted with road salt, nothing will ever
live in it again.

I hear you roll over in bed, and feel
a twinge of something
one part felicity, one part despair—
out there in the gray, the single ones,
bachelors, widows,
teen-age kids delirious
with lust and loneliness, how
do they make it through
the bludgeoning of March?
Bedsprings hail your rising,
I know your yawn, the rubbing
of eyes, feel you
warm along my withered skin—am I
saved?
We gaze at troll's dawn together, and
the first robin
flutters in to whet his beak on twigs;
his mate, clutching the filthy earth,
listens to the black black bells.

Heart of Stone

In May, the pressure on
the temples, toes: I keep
my hat on at work, in shops, at bars;
my shoes come loose and shuffle.
June: I drop disguises in
the sun, horns and hooves agleam,
kicking sand.

On an azure coast,
browning like good French bread,
we pick up pebbles on the beach.
She bends, showing white skin under
her bikini: my goat blood races.
"Look!"
It's special: red, a heart
so perfect she's sure it's carved.
Carved? By whom? And is it an old
stone, I wonder. "All stones are old,"
she murmurs in the naked wisdom
of nymphs: "It's a message."

I feel the menace tingling
in my horns.

Snorting in midnight lechery,
I fall away from the moment:
who carved the thing, red, perfect?
Some other split-hooved creature, in last
summer's sun?—the sea
has smoothed at it much longer. A monk,
then, in the dark time, praising
his long frustration to heaven? Or
maybe some passionate Goth, bleeding
guilt for a past in ruins?
This is graveyard soil; below

our seesaw bed the rocks
of Roman walls are still
intact—"All stones are old."
Well, Roman, then, my lusty
nymph, the heart of a
centurion, a slave?
I wrench at time, and cherish
skin to skin. We sleep.

In the milky light I am
already wide-eyed, wondering:
perhaps, perhaps
some tanned old Greek, tired
of getting and spending, a token for
his charming native boy? Or—
the coarse hair bristles on my spine—
Cro-Magnon himself (all stones are old)
carving his red delight
in the misty morning of man-hood?

Stop! My horns ache
with reflection—our breed is not
accustomed . . . I feel itching
in my hooves, glance at her browning
skin, stirring with easy
breathing, feel my roots
atingle, reach out
to her white breast—but
think. Think. Think again—
and steal off, click-click of hooves
on tile, to stand on pebbles,
wondering: who sent
this memory to fog
the sunny morning?

Birthday Card to My Mother

The toughness indoor people have:
  the will
to brave confusion in
mohair sofas, crocheted doilies—challenging
in every tidy corner some
bit of the outdoor drift and sag;
  the tenacity
in forty quarts of cherries up for winter,
gallon churns of sherbet at
family reunions,
fifty thousand suppers cleared away;
  the tempering
of rent-men at the front door, hanging on,
light bills overdue,
sons off to war or buried, daughters
taking on the names of strangers.

You have come through
the years of wheelchairs, loneliness—
a generation of pain
knotting the joints like ancient apple trees;
you always knew
this was no world to be weak in:
where best friends wither to old
phone numbers in far-off towns;
where the sting of children is always
sharper than serpents' teeth; where
love itself goes shifting
and slipping away to shadows.

You have survived it all,
come through wreckage and triumph hard
at the center but spreading
gentleness around you—nowhere
by your bright hearth has the dust

of bitterness lain unswept;
today, thinking back, thinking ahead
to other birthdays, I
lean upon your courage
and sign this card, as always,
with love.

Congenial Poet Desires Intense Relationship with Warm, Intelligent Poem

In the city, summer
slugs us like a bursting pillow;
feathers whisper
down our itching necks:
  SENSITIVE, LITERATE PROFESSIONAL MAN
  SEEKS ATTRACTIVE NON-CONFORMIST GIRL . . .
The long streets
sizzle
like hibachis; fans all over town
begin to whisper,
calling for help in every bus and subway:
  GAY MALE, 25, SLIM, HANDSOME,
  WANTS GOOD-LOOKING, ATHLETIC MAN IN 20'S . . .
We hold hot hands crosstown;
why is the girl in blue tennis shoes pouting,
the woman in the back of the bus
humming to someone:
  PRETTY, TRAVELED DIVORCEE, YOUTHFUL 50'S,
  SEEKS DISCRIMINATING, MATURE MAN
  FOR INTELLECTUAL STIMULATION IN DAYTIME,
  EMOTIONAL COMMITMENT AT NIGHT . . .
In this city
there is never night,
our eyelids
will not work, we sleep
watching our lives flicker
on the walls, feeling the heat close in,
hearing the whispers
rustle in the brilliant midnight parks:
  MALE, 29, ENJOYS MUSIC, TENNIS
  DESIRES VIGOROUS, REFINED WOMAN
  FOR OUTDOOR SPORTS AND BACH . . .
  CULTURED, PETITE WIDOW, GOOD DISPOSITION,

WANTS MEANINGFUL RELATIONSHIP
WITH BALANCED, CREATIVE MAN OVER 30 . . .
HEALTHY, WELL-TO-DO BACHELOR
SEEKS EROTIC LIAISON
WITH SENSUAL FREE SPIRIT . . .
In this city the whispers
roar at us:
Where there is no silence
can there be speech?
Where there is no darkness
can there be light?
In a burden of heat
can there be warmth?
In the crush of bodies
can there be feeling?

We listen
to the whispers in the air
and feel the terrible
compassion
come on like summer rain.

This Moment

Wasn't it only a day or two ago
birches were beginning to yellow—and now
rain streaks the windows and soaks
the trophies of our summer's labor, geodes,
shells, marigolds. Wet
tiles are working loose
and roofs are leaking autumn
as your touching finds again
the pity of people on subways, at public parks
in their brave summer dresses, finds
the land of inside-out: in the bedroom
your sun comes up again,
in the kitchen your nearness
turns water to wine, a telling of moments
clairvoyant as geodes,
outside plain as pudding,
inside jewels. Treasures shine
in your dazzling skin:
the shape of pears, gold
of nectarines, all
symmetries, and words
like melody, intelligence, waking, sleep.
To all the seductions of stone
you offer the gift of moments:
shadowy, hard,
immortal.

First Snow

After the long red warning of maples
it is still a surprise attack, the hordes
sweeping in at night, and at dawn
riding the shadows
as we lie in the shelter of blankets,
in the summer blood of our loving,
and feel the old terror of time
freezing the land.

The outer walls are abandoned,
the same every year, the flowers
frozen; we dig in behind the storm windows,
remembering noon in the hazy
shimmer of corn fields,
remembering noon with aspens
and far-away bells—
but each year the losses: the old ones,
limping off to their dim consummation,
tell us fear is a small brown mouse
come in from the cold to chew
at the belly nerves,
and it touches us now, the truth
of the whole gray assault: it is war
to the ultimate cold
and we lie in the shelter of blankets,
in the summer blood of our loving,
and feel the old terror of time
freezing the land.

If Martha Is a Model Mother-in-Law, She Is Definitely the Latest Model

But Martha was cumbered about
with much serving . . .
Luke 10:40

They move in the sunshine of caring,
these women whose names are never
Dulcinea or Rosalind, not even Mary,
these women in sensible shoes
whose names are always Martha:
they pad through a quilted landscape
of Bibles and potted ferns,
the tinny piano in the parlor
playing rag and Rock
of Ages to the milkman's immortal horse,
and Martha is always there, singing
lullabies to the children
and mending checkered trousers
and putting on the kettle—
and things go on like that, as if
the potted ferns were paper and
the sun were embroidered onto a muslin sky,
until this particular Martha,
come from a childhood earlier than airplanes,
young with the brand new Model T
and the women's vote, a lacy bride,
younger as Lindy hopped to Paris,
younger still with VJ Day
and men on the moon and rockets
to Mars, a lacy bride
for forty-five summers, then
watering grave chrysanthemums
on Sunday afternoons forever; after
seventy winters of starched white shirts
and ovens and diapers and needles

and pins, needles and pins, bright
with the sunshine of caring,
she's traded the horsehair loveseat in
on an air-conditioned LeSabre,
and her special daiquiris have come
a long way from lemon-
ade in the shade; she's not
looking back, this Martha, she's
holding a handful of aces, playing
dealer's choice with life.
And she isn't missing a trick.

In Two Degrees of Cold

That afternoon, you snapped a sprig
of forsythia,
put it in a glass to warm and flower.
I knew it wouldn't; winter was
too deep.

In the morning, snow came, delicate,
big flakes floating like
kids' paper cutouts; all day
the neighbors' doorways twinkled
green and red, running lights in snow.
At dusk the flakes got smaller,
businesslike, stuck
to the sides of things. Somewhere
wheels whined in the dark. The snowplow
blinked in bedroom curtains.
We shivered at far edges of the blanket.

By morning we were adrift,
boot-deep in fluff
still coming—shoveling to the street,
cursing the snowplow's ridges.
All day it whistled, even in noon thaw,
icicles dribbling from eaves.
We stayed inside, made coffee, silently
passed the papers, watched the weather
on TV, glanced across the long room at each
other, pacing,
wiped steam from windows, shoveled for the mail man,
the paper girl.
And waited.
By night the snow was wetter, finally
almost rain, freezing
where it splashed: ice and water
had forgotten which was which. In bed

we heard icicles ticking lower,
the sander rumbling past.
We burrowed into blankets
separate
and would not sleep.

It never went quite dark.
When morning lightened the white
night, the world was ice
from eaves to evergreens, houses made cages
of icicles, snow crusted
crystal-hard, to bear the weight
of kids and dogs, stiff-legged on the glare;
bushes sagged with the burden,
birches drooped, and already snow
had started piling up on ice,
the sky gone crazy, dumping the stuff
just to get rid of it, a sifted
avalanche.

The sun forgot us. Day and night
the sky was a wicked gray on gray, and always
the swirl
of feathers in the air.
Outside nothing moved:
dogs stayed in, the rabbit tracks
stopped, birds
lined the neighbor's chimney
and didn't stir.
The furnace clicked on, whirred.
We toyed with coffee, watched
each other, nervous,
holding out for thaw.

One morning, in a glass:
yellow flowers.

Economics

These are the iron laws of love:
nothing ever comes free;
there is no such thing as a bargain;
and *you never get more than you pay*
and pay
and pay for.
Blue letters in the bottom drawer:
profit and loss. And in bed
the expensive breathing,
the steadiness a faithful
whisper:
never sell out,
never sell out.

A Kind of Fruitfulness

The apple tree
is pregnant again: at ten o'clock
the sun is lighting torches
in the blossoms, in the breasts
of nesting robins—it is on us
again, the season of
beginnings; we know where it leads, the way
from a vision of toys to the fact
of thinning hair. Not
youth, not freshness, then,
not innocence: we have had
that music, know
its endings. Apple tree,
love your blossoms; but we
stand outside fertility,
trusting the gift of living:
ripeness, ripeness.

To My Late Wife

You are witching time and space,
my love,
in your race to the one o'clock plane,
the eight o'clock curtain,
calling to every fickle moment,
Linger awhile;
your dependable tardiness
is a way of wringing life
to its last hope, promising
a moratorium on death—because,
my love,
if you should die,
everything in the world would stop:
planes would sit forever
on weedy runways,
actors would pause
forever in rehearsals . . .
But of course you will not die:
you'll go on scurrying through space,
constantly making up time,
knowing we are better late
than forever.

Love in the Rain

In the primitive green of midnight
it is weather for ducks: mallards
are swimming through clover, teals
wading in crabgrass;

our thighs are as slippery as grass,
dandelions tickle our rubbery
backs as we roll, summer
stalks through the rain in our fingers;

herons stalk the deep grass
stabbing for minnows, swans
are cruising the garden, sandpipers
sway through sand;

the sky sways with the rain,
wavering shapes of trees
show us the wind: in the drizzle
our skin is a jungle fever;

it's a jungle out here, frogs
one jump ahead of the cranes,
worms waiting for cranes
in the hungry earth;

our bodies are stalking the earth
as we sway through a jungle of grass,
feeling inside us the rain
as it comes and it comes and it comes.

Scrapbook

What I remember is
  the overhead fan in Bangkok,
  turning like wheels in old movies,
  slowly backwards;
I remember
  turning to you and squinting
  as if you were shining on me.
What I remember is
  evening haze in Calcutta,
  dung firing the brass pots;
I remember
  your blondness in brown
  children: strange foreign light.
I remember
  the blind camel at Isfahan
  plodding in circles, grinding the bloody husks
  of pomegranates; and
  in the empty bazaar
  your slow step in the dark.

Do you remember
  the parting in Trieste, sunset
  slipping through bars in the station, the train
  clanging like doors of dungeons;
  and pain splitting the night
  like summer lightning?
What I remember is
  glances that looked deep,
  the touch of skin that felt bone,
  whispers out of the telling
  of the heart.
Do you remember
  in the quays and airports of our past,
  that fading Schedule of Departures,
  our belonging only to places, things—
  adrift
  inside our permanence?